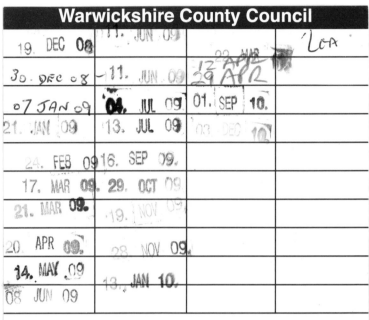

A Train is for Life

Pete Waterman

A Train is for Life

Pete Waterman

Ian Allan
PUBLISHING

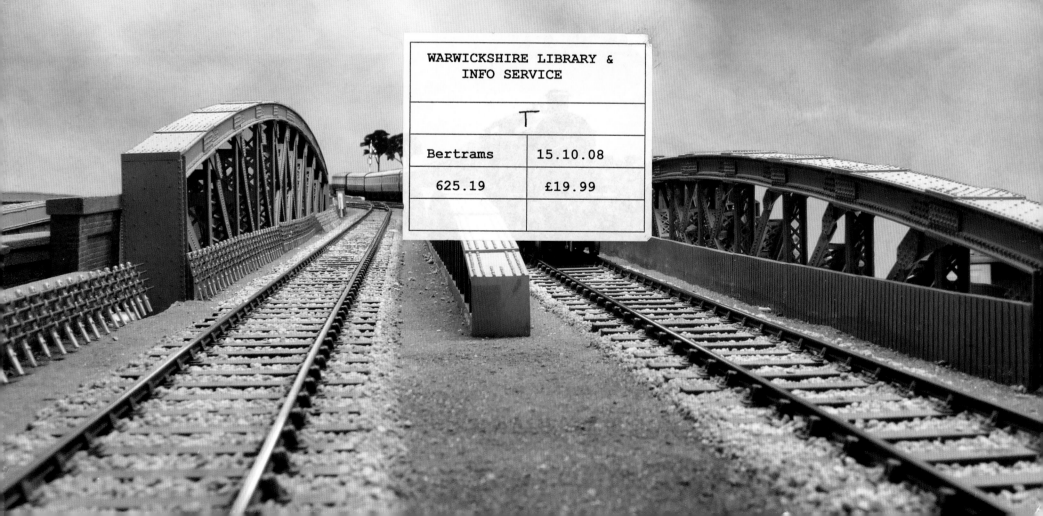

First published 2008

ISBN (10) 0 7110 3251 3
ISBN (13) 978 0 7110 3251 3

Published by Ian Allan Publishing

an imprint of Ian Allan Publishing Ltd, Hersham, Surrey, KT12 4RG

Printed in England by Ian Allan Printing Ltd, Hersham, Surrey, KT12 4RG

Code: 0810/F

Visit the Ian Allan Publishing website at www.ianallanpublishing.com

PREVIOUS PAGE: Modified 'Hall' No 6966 *Witchingham Hall* is seen approaching Leamington Spa General across the girder bridges in the town centre.

The one thing we were committed to in The Collection was to show a large variety of types. Not just steam engines but, as far as we are concerned, railway equipment of all sorts.

George Mackinnon-Ure and Geoff Holt built all of the 10mm locos, with George responsible for all of the Great Western engines and Geoff the London & North Western engines.

The technology that we use for steam engines is not practical when it comes to creating concave and convex shapes. By watching George and Geoff it was obvious that certain parts of their skills could be reproduced by computers. We have used etch technology for well over 40 years now but the leap between the technology of etch 40 years ago and today is colossal. When you think of the size of the computer that put the man on the moon, and the power of the computer needed to do modern 3D computer drawings, it is quite phenomenal. Computers still do not put the stuff together, but for the first time we can assemble the drawings in a CAD package to make sure that all the parts fit, and we can check the scale.

There is no computer that can research the prototype, and before we start anything we try and get hold of works' drawings and not use modellers' drawings. We have found that modellers' drawings are far from accurate. We will then pore over as many photographs as we can. It is important, and in fact is imperative, that you find pictures of the period you wish to model, as all railway equipment was constantly updated or renewed and unlike real railways, models can only capture one point in time. If we take, for example, 10000 and 10001, these were experimental prototypes, each being very different from the other. No 10000, sometimes in its early period, changed every 14 to 16 weeks, with parts being removed to

make the engine easier to work on. You then add changes caused by running practices, and you will see that to model these two models from 1947 to 1961 you would need eight completely different locomotives and that was certainly not feasible for us.

The other problem that we find is that you can never find the shot of the part which you particularly need, but it's sod's law that the minute you show somebody that locomotive when it is finished, they have the picture you were looking for. When building a collection like this, you must always have in mind an end game. It is doubtful whether you will ever get there, but there must be a purpose. The truth is that most things, when you see them, can find an excuse to be built. The danger with this approach is that you never achieve anything. Time is never on your side and, with the quality of George and Geoff, it is not unusual to take three to four years to build two locomotives, albeit of the same class. It is obvious that you can never build a rake of 10 coaches using the same method. Coaches are a completely separate skill.

I first met George back in the '50s at Bearwood Models where he worked in the shop and made models for customers. George started working for us in 1985 and is still sitting in his workshop creating what I believe to be some of the world's best models. I met Geoff Holt at roughly the same time. Geoff undertook the LNWR engines and the BR engines. While we built Leamington, Geoff was an inspiration and he hand built all the points. Into his 80s, he is still building locos for customers.

RIGHT: A fine summer's day with the author opening the Echills Wood Railway. What the picture doesn't tell you is that the wonderful looking 'County' driven by Pete actually ran out of steam half way around!

It was very early in the 1950s that trains became part of my life. Not just the real things but models. My Dad and my Grandad fuelled a passion in me that has lasted throughout my life. Indeed, there have been times when it has been my life, my shelter in a storm, my love in a sometimes lonely world and my stability when all around me seemed to be unravelling.

You could say that that first Bassett Lowke, brought back from Northampton by my Dad and Grandad, after they'd been to watch Coventry play there, changed the course of my life. That was way back in 1952 and since then it is true to say that there has never been a year when model engines of some sort have been far from my side. Even in the 1970s and '80s when my success in the music business took me all over the world, I would take bits of models with me so that I could build them whilst I was in hotel rooms. Difficult to imagine now, but in those days you could take a tool box on board a plane.

Still reflecting on days gone by, I remember my Mum apparently taking me to see my uncle Ernie fishing the river Leam in Leamington (I was too young to know that Aunty Ginny and Mum were actually going with him for a drink). They used to leave me on the station, in my element, and would come back later to pick me up. Can you imagine what would be said of a parent who did that today? Whereas in those days nobody blinked an eye.

So throughout the '50s I was always somewhere beside a railway, be it at my best mate Keith's, who had a Trix which kept us occupied for many hours, or in my house where my Dad built a Tri-ang train set on a board over the bath. This proved to be a bit of a problem for my Mum and my sister who quite enjoyed

having a bath but, as for me, well I can genuinely say that I spent hours in the bathroom and never had to worry about getting wet.

It was the rebuilding of Coventry Station in the late 1950s and early '60s that prompted me to start modelling. In the '50s the mags were divided into two schools: Sid Pritchard's *Railway Modeller*, whose slogan was 'for the average modeller', and *Model Railway*

ABOVE: The author and John Glaze, one of the steam boiler inspectors, making adjustments to a 5-inch gauge model of *City of Birmingham* built by David Aitken. This sat in a solicitors' office and then in the Crewe Museum before being returned to working order.

News which, although nowhere near the quality of the *Modeller,* carried the best features for the young modeller who wanted to do more than play with a train set, and whose aim was to try and get that model to look something like the real thing.

In the mid 1950s two people's names stand out for me: Norris and Beeston. The Norris layout photos were just unbelievable. The locomotives, built by Bernard Miller, were just magnificent and the photos of Stan Beeston's locos — built for this or that colonel – well, they were the pinnacle of perfection and just took my breath away. It is quite something, as I look back all those years, to be able to say with certainty that my passion for modelling has never abated although I accept that I have been very fortunate to be in a position to do what I do.

I can remember the earful I used to get from my Mum when I came home with a bit of scrap loco, or just plain black from playing. What would she say now I wonder, if she could see all the steam engines the Trust owns or see that I have my own railway works and model train company? But then again, she would have never gotten over the shock of me becoming 'a doctor', and two times over at that.

My model collection started back in 1958 and I still have some of those, but this book is about the bigger models and that means 7mm and over.

The defining moment for me was seeing, in the flesh, the models of Guy Williams for Pendon. I visited the railway in the late 1960s and was made very welcome and I started friendships with modellers that I had only previously read about. Most of the people that I met at that time were getting on in years, indeed only a young Tony Reynolds was about my age. But it

ABOVE: The backbone of any model railway based on the West Midlands has to be the Stanier 'Black 5s'. This is a hand-built 7mm loco by Vic Green.

was through Guy that I met up with Ron Cadman, and the local model shop owner in Coventry, Barry Jones, and together we formed Models & Leisure. This brought me into contact with all the great names that I had only previously heard about.

Even at this stage, real skills were being allowed to fade under the guise of progress and those who were pushing to 'make things better' were swamped in a sea of mediocrity. The argument that price was the barrier was too easy a cop out for me, since I have seen too many high cost, low quality models. It broke my heart to see highly skilled workers being hampered by price so I made up my mind to resurrect the true skills of the industry and, in doing so, ensure that we would show future generations that we had the best models in the world. To this end I set up WHRT — the Waterman Railway Heritage Trust.

Since the early 1980s we have sponsored, not only the restoration of steam and diesel engines, but also electrics and modelling skills. So here is a tribute to those guys. We can't cover all the collection and neither would we want to, because we still like going to shows and showing people what we are doing.

I've left the choice of photos to the publishers and you will notice that there are no chapters and few words but this is not a book about railways – it's a book about modellers.

Railways still play a major part in my life and over the last 10 years, I, together with a few fellow enthusiasts, have built what was a small idea into a major servicing facility in Crewe. Although part of the building dates from 1880, the rest of the site is absolutely 'state of the art'. We also have a very large heavy repair shop in Crewe, where we specialise in steam and where we always have more than 15 boilers in at any one time. To date, our most prestigious claim to fame was the restoration of the LMS 'Super D'. The Trust owns mainly Great Western engines that can be seen on most preserved lines. Over the years, I have made many friends in the railway industry and I count myself lucky to have been in the privileged position of being able to see the railway, not only as an enthusiast but as a wonderful industry. It seems ironic to think that after 50 years of neglect, people are just waking up to the fact that railways are a brilliant idea! I don't think that I will be around to see the High Speed Trains of the next generation, but for the first time, they do

look more than just a pipe dream — I hope so.
I would like to thank the following people for their help with this book:

- Tony Wright who, for the last 10 years, has been taking photographs and who took the majority of photos in this book.
- The staff at Ian Allan for their perseverance and enthusiasm.
- Viv for putting my words into English.
- And especially to Helen for her patience — she almost got to the point of screaming!

The book is meant to be a pictorial feast of my collection over the years. This has taken me 50 years of my life to collect — let's hope that a Part 2 will reflect the next 50!

So sit back and wonder at these modellers and let's lift a glass to them all and thank God for the skill they brought to railway modelling.

Pete Waterman
July 2008

To find out more about Pete Waterman's railway models please visit the website for his company Just Like the Real Thing (www.justliketherealthing.co.uk). From there you will also find links for his Leamington Spa model layout and The Waterman Railway Heritage Trust.

RIGHT: 'We Three Kings': A line up of three 'Kings' that are all different. Even the double chimneys are different. They are all built by Paul Hanna and painted by Conrad Cooper.

The London, Midland & Scottish Railway 'Jubilees' were certainly not strangers to me in the early 1950s. In fact, living in the West Midlands, I was able to see the 'Jubilees' every time I went spotting. The crazy thing was that we took these engines as mundane and yet here we are, 50 years later, realising that they were anything but! A cross between LMS and Great Western styles, these engines built by Stanier are beautifully balanced and, to me - in their BR Brunswick Green livery — stunning! It goes without saying that, in my opinion, to run any layout based around the West Midlands you can never have too many 'Jubilees'!

THIS PAGE: No 45595 *Southern Rhodesia* was built by David Baker from Manchester. It's a DJH kit with many refinements. It has Alan Harris wheels and is painted by Alan Brackenbrough. This engine represents really the last years of its life when it had AWS (Automatic Warning System) apparatus fitted. Although this was always a Northern engine, we regularly saw it on the West Coast main line, particularly around Cup Final days – and, yes, there were teams other than Manchester United who made the Cup Final in those days!

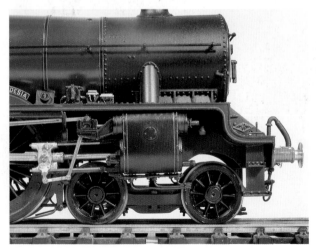

ABOVE: This superb picture says everything, I believe, about the 'Jubilees'. Note also the engine carries the electric warning flashes on the firebox.

Living in Coventry had its advantages and disadvantages. One of its major disadvantages was its distance from the Southern Region, hence there are few Southern engines in the collection – not because we have no interest, but there is only so much that any collection can achieve. In 1955 I did take a trip in my first London taxi which took me from Euston to Waterloo and I can still almost see the platform and hear the noise of Waterloo station to this day! In fact, that memory lingers longer and is more vivid than the arrival at Euston — but then again, I have visited Euston many times since. And why did we visit Waterloo? Yes, you've guessed it; we were going to the South Coast and Hayling Island where the summer holiday was spent collecting lizards, matchbox tops and sitting at the station watching these beautiful little engines. My friend Keith arrived with his parents in a car — thank God we couldn't afford a car!

RIGHT: This model came into the collection and is quite stunning. So many times I have been tempted to paint it black, which is how I remember it, but then the green London & South Western Railway livery is so lovely that we felt it appropriate to leave it alone. I know nothing about who built it or where it came from, other than it was picked up over 20 years ago in some sort of deal.

The 'Manors' were fabulous little engines and although I saw all of them, I can say that I never got bored with them. Seeing a 'Manor' with '7' on the back was just brilliant! I have fired them many times and they are an absolute delight. Built in two batches, the first by the GWR and the second by BR, they were probably perfect for the Northern Division of the Great Western. In fact, it was due to this class that I started my career in the railways. It was a foggy, late November day at Wolverhampton Stafford Road and there, sitting very forlornly, slightly bent after an accident, was 7822. With the reassurance from a fellow spotter that it had been withdrawn and was about to be cut up, together with the availability of a spanner, the smokebox number soon found its way into my duffle bag! Fast forward to a knock on the door and a policeman asking could he have the plate back as well as all the other shed plates that adorned my wall! After the caution, the judge decided that as part of my rehabilitation I should make tea for the guys at Stafford Road every Saturday morning! I also got a pass from BR to travel on the train for six weeks to get there — seemed like a good deal to me! And so it was, then, that when I left school the first job I had was at Stafford Road as a boilersmith — not my wisest choice of careers since within four years there wouldn't be any steam engines!

ABOVE: The recurring theme that you will see throughout this book — and I make no apologies for it — is that I do like railway engines in black! Although, as Tony Reynolds once said, green engines fetch more money! BR mixed traffic black with the lion on the wheel with red nameplates and number plates — and there were not as many examples of these as people think — was perfection to me. This engine, No 7819 *Hinton Manor*, is a Mitchell Kit which was built by Norman Blackburn in the North East and was painted and lined by Alan Brackenbrough. The photo is taken on the Leamington Spa coaling stage, which was built by Norman Solomon.

GWR 'Grange'

The 'Granges' were hugely successful engines and one could say they were admired by both crews and shed staff. They could be seen throughout the railway system and were used for just about anything. Sadly, and it is hard to believe this, not one of them was preserved. One would have been perfect for today's preserved railway scene.

BELOW AND OPPOSITE: No 6837 *Forthampton Grange* was built by Norman Blackburn from a Mitchell Kit and painted by Alan Brackenbrough.

Now then, there were big engines and then there were these engines! I remember seeing these with my cousin on the Midland main line, pulling what seemed to be an endless amount of coal wagons. By any stretch of the imagination, these were impressive machines. Yes, I know they had small axle boxes and the Midland probably mucked about with them too much as they were never as successful as they promised, but just standing by the side of one of these at Rugby Shed was too much! I even got to stand on the footplate! They were massive in every way. What people mistake about these engines is that they were not mechanically fired. The contraption on the tender was a rotating bunker that allowed the coal to be shaken forward. No wonder firemen were small blokes! Try telling the fireman of one of these, with a hundred wagons on the back full of coal, that steam railways were magical!

RIGHT: This is the loco part — or is it the boiler? Anyway, it's the most important part — the bit that makes it work!

THIS PAGE: Photos can only give you a glimpse of the workmanship that's gone into this engine model. Built by Geoff Holt, with wheels by Mark Wood, and standing over 3ft long, this really is some model. This is a Gauge 1 locomotive and was built by Geoff as a one-off. These pictures also demonstrate the fabulous weathering jobs that one of the finest exponents of this art, Brian Caldicott, has done. This is to me where modelling and collecting differ. This is a model of an engine that has worked hard for its living. Poor old Geoff nearly had a heart attack when he saw what we'd done to his loco but he now understands that it actually enhances even his skill.

The ultimate GWR tank engine! Which model railway of the West Midlands does not have one of these? The 0-4-2 wheel arrangement was always a GW preferred option and the '1400s', originally '48xxs', followed in that tradition. They were Collett's modern version of the '517s'. The truth about Collett really is that he was a very conservative engineer and arguably nothing he ever did was innovative. He just modernised. We saw loads of these around the Midlands and I spent many hours riding up and down Leamington Spa shed on one of these. They sometimes were in lined green when they worked prestigious branches — most were auto fitted. I know these engines very well as we have worked on the preserved versions and are currently about to start a major overhaul of a '14xx'.

ABOVE: This is an NPD kit with Harris wheels, built and painted by Peter Rolls. The photo shows just what a fabulously simple design these little engines were.

The coal tanks were a tank version of the London & North Western Railway's very successful coal engines. Crewe works did not believe in building flowery engines. Webb was a down-to-earth practical engineer with strict budgetary control. You could say Crewe 'did what they said on the box'! The coal tanks lasted right into the BR period, the last one being finally scrapped at Crewe in the mid '50s. They were used very much on branch lines, particularly around the West Midlands. The wheels were a very distinctive London & North Western feature, which were given the characteristic 'H' spoke name simply because the spokes are in the shape of an 'H'! They were actually bolted to the rims, unlike on many of the other railways.

THIS PAGE: No 588 is a 10mm loco built by Geoff Holt, painted by Brian Badger, and is in full LNWR livery.

The LNWR was an early believer in standardisation so all these engines were variations on a theme. The locomotive fitted with the coal rails had slide valves, the other has the more efficient piston type. There was a tank version of the 'DX Goods' which became known as the 'Watford Tanks', because of their use on the line to Watford.

THIS PAGE AND OPPOSITE: These 10mm 'Watford Tanks' show two versions: one with coal rails and one without and the latter has the original Ramsbottom smokebox door. Both were built by Geoff Holt and painted by Brian Badger.

The Great Central Railway was the last great railway built in Britain and went straight through the Warwickshire countryside at Rugby, on a high level flyover. I never saw many Great Central engines until probably preservation days and I certainly never saw one of these engines, designed by Gorton.

THIS PAGE AND OPPOSITE: This is a 10mm-wide steam model built by probably the best live steam builder, Dave Bracknell. It has Mark Wood wheels and is painted and lined by Alan Brackenbrough. It runs on methylated spirit and will give a good 25 minutes' running time — and it runs as beautifully as it looks. Originally, this engine was bought to run at Robert

Head's Shifnal garden set-up and many hours were spent with it on sunny days in Bob's garden. It was great fun until after lunch, by which time a large amount of Scotch had been consumed and, for no reason, the engine got stuck in the middle of the lake on Bob's scale model of Saltash Bridge!

Diesel Electric 10000/10001

Some maintain that there can be a divide between the steam modeller and the diesel modeller — not me, I just love railways! And now we come to the 10000/01 which were the first British main line diesels. To me they are absolutely stunning! The 10000 was introduced in 1946 by the LMS and the 10001 in 1948 under BR and could still be seen in the 1960s. They were a combination of steam railway technology and the ship industry. In fact, if you look closely inside, they are quite submarine like. They ran past my door on more than one occasion and throughout the 1950s I saw them almost every day. I remember them so well as a pair in black and green but to me, when they were painted in the green with a mid-white band, they became spectacular! If only I could have had the money then to preserve one of these. It seems incredible that in an age when we see eight or nine of other classes preserved, that we never kept one of the two most important engines.

THIS PAGE AND OPPOSITE: The photos of 10000 show it in its original condition, as it would have run till about 1962. The LMS lettering was removed quite early in the BR period. The thing that was difficult to achieve on this model was the fact that it was a prototype; the 10000 was constantly changing and sometimes only ran in one condition for less than a year. The photos of 10001 overleaf show it as running post-1958 and you will notice from the photos that the roofs are completely different, as are the body sides. It has also been fitted with water apparatus which allowed the water tanks to be topped up *en route*. The 10000 was also treated at the same time. The 10001 lasted long enough to actually receive a small yellow warning panel on the front.

BR '9F'

The '9F' was probably one of the finest designs of the nationalised railway! Many a time have I seen these engines travelling upwards of 65mph. They were, of course, designed for ease of maintenance and comfort for the crews. Their 10 small driving wheels gave them a huge tractive effort. One could argue that they should never have been built for some had relatively short careers. The last engine ever built by BR was named *Evening Star* and it was built at Swindon. In point of fact, *Evening Star* was also the name of the first ever engine ever to be built at Swindon.

BELOW: The loco is a DGH Kit with Alan Harris wheels, built by David Baker and painted and lined by Alan Brackenbrough. As you can see from these photos, we have kept this model of *Evening Star* in pristine condition as we use it to run Specials.

THIS PAGE: Some called the '9Fs' 'spaceships' because of the high-mounted boiler and all of the outside pipework. All this made for very easy maintenance.

The big thing in the '50s was the iron ore trains that came up from Banbury on their way to Bilston, returning with the empties, which is why I would make a bee-line for Leamington. They were not long, six to eight wagons, but weighed a vast amount and always needed a big engine. We always saw 2-8-0 '28xx','38xx' or '42xx' tanks but by the late '50s the '9Fs' replaced these and there were two kept on shed at Banbury. This what the '9Fs' really looked like: Banbury's No 92150, built for us by DJH and painted and weathered by Steve Naylor.

THIS PAGE: No 92204 is a scratch built engine by Vic Green. It is a lot cleaner than the other '9Fs' and has a different style of tender. We have had to put brand-new rods on this engine as the original ones wore out.

During the late 1920s/early '30s every railway experimented with ways to make the steam engine far more efficient (because the truth is that steam engines are highly inefficient — you lose far more steam than you use). *Fury*, built by the LMS, was one of those experiments and like most such experiments it was unsuccessful. It was later rebuilt into a look-alike 'Royal Scot' class but it always differed from all of the rest because of its origin.

THIS PAGE AND OPPOSITE: *Fury* is built by Geoff Holt and painted by Brian Badger and, yes, it actually ran in this livery.

The GWR 'Cities' were the epitome of the 4-4-0s. One hundred years ago these were the premier express engines of their day and were famous for pulling the well-known boat trains. There is something so elegant about these engines. They were designed by Churchward to do a job – and boy, did they do a job! Arguments will go on for the rest of time as to whether or not *City of Truro* ever did 100mph but who cares — we are lucky enough to be able to see one of these magnificent machines in all its glory because of this.

THIS PAGE AND OPPOSITE: These photos show you one of our 7¼ inch models built by David Aitken. The photographs show you all the details of the model, and there is not a lot more one can say about it. If it's on the original, it's on this model. Like everything else David does, it's absolutely perfect. You can see also, looking inside at the proportions of the cab, that you'd have to wear some pretty thick clothing in the winter because standing on that footplate at 90mph, with the wind whistling off the sea, must have been pretty freezing.

The straight frame 'Saints' carried the names of ladies and, of course, coming from Coventry, *Lady Godiva* had to be for us. These were the forerunners of many 4-6-0s which would follow and it is obvious when you see the 'Lady' class that Churchward was still in the early stages. Compare these with the 'Saints' later in the book. Of particular interest in this class, from a modelling point of view, is the lack of space between the first and second driving wheels. The real thing that interests me about building these locos is the research that you have to undertake. The 'Saint' class is broken down to three main groups: 'Ladies', 'Saints' and 'Courts'. There is a major difference between existing information and photos. All the information states that the first two batches, ie 'Ladies' and 'Saints', were built with their cylinder centres two and half inches about the wheel centres. We always use as many photos as we can before we start any loco project. We spend hours poring over them. What we found was that the photos do not agree with the information. Photos show us that very quickly these were brought into line with standard GWR loco practice. In fact, the information states that the last batch, the 'Courts', were built like this. So why is there no record of the change?

THIS PAGE AND OPPOSITE: This 10mm model, built by George McKinnon-Ure with Alan Harris wheels, is fully double lined by Alan Brackenbrough and is absolutely stunning! The pictures in the book of the 'Saints', 'Ladies' and Atlantics are probably the epitome of model making.

St David, the last 'Saint' in BR service, is looking the worse for wear! It is built by George McInnon-Ure, painted by Alan Brackenbrough and weathered by Brian Caldicott.

This is how the model looked before it was painted and what we have to remember is this is all created from a flat sheet of nickel silver — all marked out by hand.

The 'Counties' were the last of the Great Western engine designs and were designed by Hawksworth. They were comprised of a lot of the same features that Hawksworth had used in his 'Modified Halls'. The boiler was based around the firebox of the LMS '8F' that the GWR had built during the Second World War.

THESE PAGES AND OVERLEAF: 'County' No 1005 is probably the most historic engine in the collection. Recently purchased, it was built 1945-50 by J. P. Richards for the layout. The model is outstanding and given when it was built is as accurate as any model locomotive can be. It's tender driven, can pull anything we put behind it and was built to 7mm fine scale – and, yes, that was in 1950! And the bonus is, it's painted in real Great Western green.

THIS PAGE: No 1028 *County of Warwick* is built by Norman Blackburn, painted by Alan Brackenborough and weathered by Martyn Welch. A strange fact of the 'Counties' is that of all the classes where people have bought original nameplates or numberplates, there are apparently only two private collectors who have both for these locomotives. The question must be asked, 'Why?', as it has been easy to get the complete set for any other Great Western engine class. To purchase a set of 'County' plates was the Trust's most expensive undertaking.

It's hard to imagine now but once upon a time main line steam locomotives only had one driving wheel. These singles were built by Webb at Crewe. They were incredibly successful engines and were quite regularly double headed on Crewe to Euston runs. During this period you had to be posh to travel for there was nowhere near the amount of traffic there is today. There are many famous stories of the feats of these engines. They were always painted in Blackberry Black.

THIS PAGE: No 184 *Problem* — or in this case 'no problem'.

OPPOSITE: This is a scale 7 model built for The Collection by James Harwood in New Zealand. This is a completely scratch-built loco with everything having been handmade by James, whose real job is making special appliances for disabled people. Without a doubt, James is amongst the top modellers in the world. You will see various examples of his work but just look at the beauty that these photos show. An ex-pat who has certainly managed to capture a special part of British history!

ABOVE: No 762 *Locke* was built by Geoff Holt and painted by Brian Badger.

Leamington Layout

When we were considering building a layout, it was always going to have to be the West Midlands because that's where we grew up. Leamington Spa was absolutely ideal as we have always wanted to challenge the concept of railway modelling and we did not want to be able to view the whole layout at one time. We wanted, like the real thing, to peek in between buildings. Leamington, having viaducts through the town centre, was the perfect location. Also, it gave us the opportunity to run both Midland and Western region — there being two stations — and it also helped that it was on a curve. We didn't want any real straights. It is doubtful whether we will ever finish the layout — that is not the aim! It's the challenge of doing something well.

THIS PAGE AND OPPOSITE: These photographs show a '38xx' on a standard coal train of the '50s. There are 58 loaded wagons in this train and it is shown on Hatton Bank. The repeater signal is for the up line. The grass is made from teddy bear fur, hand cut, dyed and set fire to.

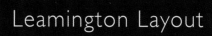

ABOVE: Hatton Bank.

LEFT: Waiting to leave on the Hatton Bank.

Leamington Layout

THIS PAGE AND OPPOSITE: These photographs show BR Standard Class 5 No 73069 at the head of a freight train and GWR King Class No 6021 *King Richard II* heading an express passenger train. The new order is shown by a BR Class 40 No D210 *Empress of Britain* and BR Class 44 No D1 *Scafell Pike*.

'3F' is the locomotives power classification, with 1 being the lowest and 9 being the most powerful. At first sight, one could be confused between the '2F', '3F' and '4F' locomotives since they were all a standard Midland Railway design and looked superficially the same. The Midland Railway had three basic power bands for its goods traffic. The Class 4s were for heavy coal trains — possibly double headed — the '3s' for intermediate traffic and '2s' for light traffic. There were lots of '3Fs' in the Midland Division and they quite regularly sat at New Street for long periods, where the spotters got to know both them and their crews very well. If you were lucky, you regularly got a lift back on one of the station pilots to Saltly in one of the cabs. Not so powerful looking as the '4s', the '3s' mainly retained their Johnson tenders, which was always how you could tell, at a distance, that it wasn't a '4'.

THIS PAGE AND OPPOSITE: These pictures show the Eric Underhill Kit, built by David Baker and painted by Alan Brackenbrough. The '3Fs' are simple little models at home on any size layout.

THIS PAGE AND OPPOSITE: A work-stained '3F' built by
Eric Underhill and weathered by Brian Caldicott.

After 10000/1 had been heavily trialled, the first diesels to be built by BR as part of its Modernisation Plan were what became known to us all as the 'Peaks' and were numbered D1-10. They were, in fact, generally similar to 10000/1 but the bogies were from the Southern Region experimental diesels 10201-3. They had Sulzer power units and had discs on the front to denote train classification. Steam boilers were provided as the trains that these diesels were designed to pull still had steam heating. You can see footsteps on the side where the fireman would have climbed on the roof to put the bag in.

ABOVE: D1 *Scafell Pike* was built at MM1 for us and shows the loco as it would have appeared when it entered service. I can still see the day when D1 first appeared at Birmingham New Street on a test run. It was met with boos and cheers. I cheered! The Trust had a real Class 46 (as the class was renumbered) at one time.

OPPOSITE: The doors on the front of the cab were meant to allow the crews to change while the train was on the move but it never worked and always made for a draughty cab.

It's hard to look back to that early 1950s period and be able to understand the decision of the BR Board to carry on the design of certain prewar types. One of these was the BR 2-6-0 Standard 2s because essentially they were pure LMS Ivatt design, almost carbon copies, but having said that, if a design works, why change it? Under BR they were built at more than one workshop.

THIS PAGE AND OPPOSITE TOP: This is a DJH kit and is one of a couple we have had built for us by DJH. Weathered by Steve Naylor, they work quite regularly on short pick-up trains.

TOP RIGHT AND RIGHT: This is the second DJH-built kit, again weathered by Steve Naylor.

The 'B1s' were, without a doubt, my personal favourite LNER engine. (I have to be very careful here, looking after as many LNER 'A4s' as we do!) They are magnificently balanced engines and were equally at home on passenger or freight duties. For an engineering company based at Crewe, we seem to be doing more Doncaster engines than anything else at the moment. We are becoming quite expert at Gresley engineering, which gives me fabulous excuses with my camera to see parts of these locos in my own workshops that the modeller doesn't ever get to see. When you work on these boilers you can say that LNER had a very different view of their value then the GWR/LMS. They are almost agricultural in build, by comparison! We regularly saw these engines through the Midlands on the Great Central and at Woodford Halse. It also was not unusual to see them at Leamington.

THIS PAGE AND OPPOSITE: This engine is a Piercy kit, built for us by DJH with some extra detail. Although we love 'B1s' it is doubtful whether No 61073 ever made it as far as Leamington Spa but, on my rake of blood and custard-liveried Gresley coaches, who cares! We could be anywhere! We are about to start work on overhauling the real 'B1' – a great time to get photographs of the parts you normally don't see.

The 'B1s' had a very funny smokebox door arrangement and are hard to model but the Piercy kit got it perfectly. These kits were quite ahead of their time when they first came out.

One of the Southern engine classes I regularly saw in my few days spotting there, was the 'Schools', and what magnificent engines they were. I saw them both in mixed traffic, black and green. The 'Schools' would regularly get to Oxford on inter-Regional trains and although probably would have been rare visitors to Leamington, one could always stretch a point!

THIS PAGE AND OPPOSITE: Painted and lined by Alan Brackenbrough, this model, No 30914 *Eastbourne*, is one of a pair built for us. It has Alan Harris wheels and runs as good as it looks. This is an engine I use regularly on the layout because it is a joy!

What people tend to forget is that at some point even Swindon couldn't cope with the demand for new locomotives and had to purchase some of them from outside. A cancelled order at Beyer's in Manchester led the GWR to buy what became known as the 'Beyer Goods', which were basically in the same power classification as the 'Armstrong Goods'/'Dean Goods'.

They were unusual for GW engines in that they had curved running plates, almost Midland-like in appearance. They were then fitted with GW fittings, making them look very pretty. They were obviously slightly unusual in that their boilers were not standard, so had limited lifespans.

THIS PAGE AND OPPOSITE: No 337 is a David Aitken 7¼in live steam model. As the photos show, this is an unusual model and always stops people in their tracks. Just look at the cab detail and the work involved on the inside motion. Transfers were made by us as nobody had ever gone into this much detail before. On first glance, it looks like a 'Dean Goods' and when people hear the history of what it is, they are smitten.

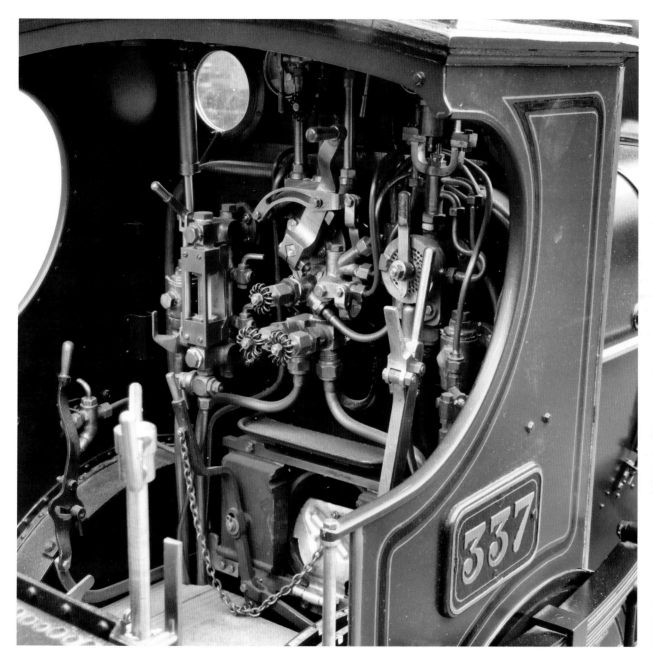

Coaches are essential, of course, on a railway, but they are a subject all of their own. You have to remember that the railways are built on a class system and the railway shortens or abbreviates everything. In the period that we are modelling, trains did not run in fixed rakes but were assembled for individual trains. In the original carriage there would have been diagram books and when the trains were assembled, the schedule would list the passenger class type, ie a 1st Class coach would have been given the initial 'F', a 2nd Class 'S' (not standard), and a 3rd Class 'T' (this is what we now class as standard). When a carriage had a mix of classes it was referred to as a 'C' — composite. At the front, and/or back, of a train there was a brake vehicle, classified with the letter 'B'. The original coaches from the turn of the 20th century had corridors, and they were given the letter 'K'. The inter-war years saw the introduction of open coaches, represented by the letter 'O', and suburban coaches which had no corridors had the letters 'NC'. So a typical train up to the late 1950s for the Western Region would be a BTK, CK, TK, TO, BFK or BCK. If that sounds complicated, the LMS used a different system! So you can see, coaches become a very difficult subject, but they are essential for any railway.

THIS PAGE: A 'toplight' BCK built by us, for us, and painted by Conrad Cooper. Known as Blood and Custard, Crimson and Cream or Carmine and Cream, they were the standard BR colours in the 1950s. The Maroon livery replaced these schemes from 1957 onwards/

OPPOSITE: These pictures on this page show a toplight brake composite, a BCK, and a composite, a CK, in full Great Western livery, built by us and painted by Conrad Cooper.

LMS 'Black 5'

The 'Stanier 5s', 'Black 5s' or 'Mickeys' were the engine you saw most of if you lived in the West Midlands. There seemed a never ending stream of them, some in pretty grotty condition. But they were the mainstay of everyday passenger traffic. I don't remember ever getting that excited when I saw one, but they are without a doubt perfectly designed engines for the job to be done. We had many of these shedded at Rugby, so if you hadn't got a book full of numbers at the end of the day, a quick run round there would soon top you up. The '5s' were equally at home right across Britain and you were as likely to see one on the Western as on the Midland. A pair of 'Black 5s' was even kept to pull the Royal Train.

THIS PAGE AND OPPOSITE: No 44874 was built by Vic Green from scratch. It has scratch-built wheels and the cab detail is quite astonishing. The model is at some point to be re-wheeled as soon as we get a set of Alan Harris wheels.

BR 'Standard 5'

The 'Standard 5s' were BR's version of the 'Black 5' with some modern features: the footplate was raised for easy access to oiling; self-cleaning smokeboxes and rocker grates. The cabs were exceptionally well laid out and the locomotives are absolutely delightful to drive. This was probably one of the very few times in the history of railway design that the actual end user was ever consulted. These engines could carry different tenders depending on the region of initial allocation.

THESE PAGES: This engine came out of a conversation with Dave Baker in his garden one summer evening. An unmade kit Dave no longer wanted and a set of Alan Harris wheels needed a home. So, we designed a chassis for the loco and did the parts for Dave. No 73069 was always a Leamington Spa engine. Painted by Alan Brackenborough, he pushed the painting to the limit by applying the shed name to the bufferbeam. Stunning!

Now, we could spend a long time going through the nuances of diesels, because I can assure you they are more complicated than you think. But without getting too technical we will look at the Class 24s and 25s here. In the Modernisation Plan of 1955 the railway followed its own standard practice of putting locomotives in order of power classifications — Class 1 to 5, or Types when it referred to the diesels. The Modernisation Plan called for Types of diesels from 1 to 4 and identified the jobs that these locomotives would be suitable for. (I don't intend to have a debate here whether it got it right or wrong, it's what they did). The Type 2s, of which there were to be a large number, were seen by BR as being the standard short-haul freight locomotive. It didn't really envisage that rapid decline in this market would almost make the type redundant before it had been built. Like everything else in the Modernisation Plan, it was expected that changes would be made as experience was gained. The first of the Class 24s went into service on the Southern Region. What follows are photographs of the engines as they developed from 1958 to the '80s.

THIS PAGE AND OPPOSITE: No 24150 represents the second type of Class 24, with a headcode box and no horns. The skirting has been removed from the sides and it is painted in BR standard blue livery.

BR Class 24 and 25

TOP: These pictures show a Class 25 as built with headcode box and horns in standard green livery as would have been delivered in 1960s. The skirting was now not part of the main body work. Compare this with the Class 24 in the previous pictures — you will see it has different water tanks and fuel tanks.

BOTTOM: This shows the ultimate Class 25 with no side grills. This engine is owned by the trust and was the last engine ever built by Beyer Peacock in Manchester and the last engine ever delivered to BR in the two-tone green livery. This loco is currently on loan to West Coast Railways and will be returning to main line use. One day we may see that once familiar sight in the West Midlands of two 'Rats' to Rhyl!

ABOVE: This shows the standard Class 24 as it was when it entered service in 1958, with skirts along the side. The first six as delivered to the Southern were unique, as they had a white band down the middle.

RIGHT: This shows the Class 24 cab (left) and the Class 24/1 cab (right). You will notice head codes and the body side skirts have been removed.

THIS PAGE: Class 25/1 — it all goes to show that diesels are not as simple as they seem.

The Great Western at the Grouping in 1924 took over all of the railways in south Wales. South Wales was famous for its pits and it shipped much of the coal it mined to the empire from docks in or around the area. The railway system, which ran through deep valleys, called for very strong, sturdy engines. At the Grouping GWR found itself with a huge amount of engines of the 0-6-2T type. The south Wales companies found that this type of loco was best suited to the valleys. But by the time they reached the GWR they were well and truly worn out. So Collett, the GWR's Chief Mechanical Engineer, decided to replace these with his own 0-6-2T, the '56xx' class. Earlier in this book I have stated that Collett was not really an innovator, and this class proves it. The '56s', although hugely powerful engines, as built, were an embarrassment. They fell off the track on regular occasions and were indifferent steamers. Anybody who has worked on these and the '14xxs', can instantly see Stanier's hand at work in the latter. So much of what became standard on LMS engines was first tried by Stanier on these engines. One can well imagine that Stanier didn't think much of Collett's design and when the CME job was offered at the LMS he couldn't wait to leave.

RIGHT AND OPPOSITE: No 6634 is one of the Leamington engines, built, painted and weathered by Graham Bone, and is seen on the coaling stage. Leamington also has a green lined version. The trust also owns one of the real engines, which carries an ex-'Bulldog' boiler.

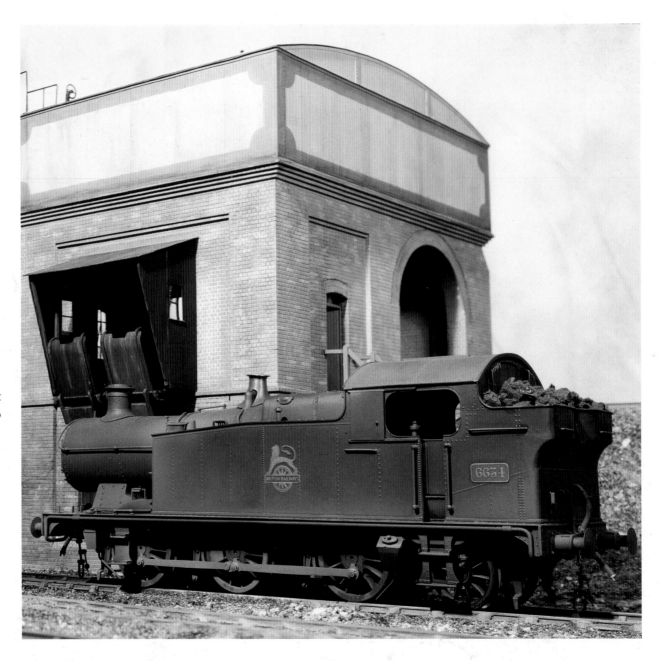

GWR '56xx' 0-6-2T

Built and weathered by Graham Bone, this shows the '66' in absolutely super condition for the 1950s/early '60s.

Built by Paul Hanna, painted by Conrad Cooper and weathered by Martyn Welch, this is one of the lined green versions which we have at Leamington.

When the GWR needed to build its most powerful engine it could not have chosen a better name than the 'Kings'. They were the most powerful 4-6-0 in Britain when built and the heaviest engines on the Great Western. This severely restricted their route availability but luckily Paddington-Wolverhampton was one of their routes and I spent many hours on the 'Kings', seeing all of them more than once. For our Leamington model layout, 'Kings' rule, as we would have seen at least one on nearly every express. Luckily for us, 'Kings' are well preserved and can still be seen regularly on the main line. One difference to look out for is that the 'Kings' carried four different types of chimney.

RIGHT: This is how I remember first seeing the 'Kings' — in the light blue, with the blood and custard coaches. The engine was built by Paul Hanna, painted and lined by Conrad Cooper, and the coaches were built and painted by myself, lined by Conrad Cooper. They are seen on an up express on Hatton Bank.

OPPOSITE: A low-angle view of No 6004 *King George II* Notice how neat the ballast is. Also, how the track is weathered.

THIS PAGE AND OPPOSITE TOP LEFT: *King Edward III,*
No 6022, of Wolverhampton has the flat-sided double
chimney and lubricator, showing all the variations that the
'Kings' actually had. Built by Paul Hanna, it was painted by
Conrad Cooper.

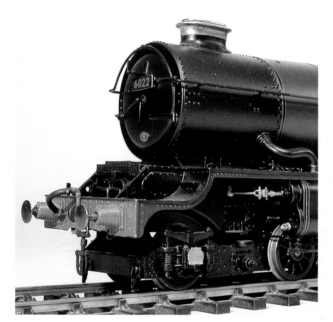

ABOVE AND LEFT: This shows 'King' No 6005 *King George II* with its single chimney, in early '50s livery. Built by Paul Hanna, painted by Conrad Cooper, it shows the full size of these engines.

ABOVE AND OPPOSITE: These photographs shows No D222 *Laconia* as it entered service. This was regularly seen around the Midlands and I travelled behind it so many times. The loco is a JLTRT kit, built by Roger Manton and painted and weathered by him. We have the original nameplates in our collection.

LEFT: No D210 *Empress of Britain* is a JLTRT kit and is painted and built by the factory. It was the first one of the class I ever saw and I regularly travelled behind it. We also have the name plate in the collection.

The Type 4s were the first big diesels to enter service in large numbers. They first went to the Eastern Region out of Liverpool Street but it was not long before the West Coast succumbed to the whistle of the turbos. Made by Vulcan in Newton-le-Willows and named after liners, they made mincemeat of a lot of the old steam jobs. They can be draughty and the noise can get to you after a bit, but then is anything perfect? I started collecting the plates of the Class 40s as they came up for sale. I still think of these on the West Coast racing through Brinklow on a summer evening as I sat fishing with my dad. I have been on these all over the regions, and for me, still today, they are top of the pops!

The early Type 4 diesels developed into the Class 40s could be seen all over the system, particularly in the later days, but Swindon was a regular hunting ground for enthusiasts. Probably the most famous part of Swindon was the wall of 'A' Shop. This is John Dorman's beautiful model of the Swindon 'A' Shop. The picture was taken at one of the Swindon exhibitions with the sunlight streaming through the windows of the real 'A' Shop. So, you could say, this is as close as we could get to the real thing.

THIS PAGE AND OPPOSITE: I have broken all the rules to include these three photos. This is not my engine, although it is a JLTRT kit; it wasn't built by us and it's not even on our layout, but everything in these photographs is what modelling is about to me. The engine was built and painted by Brian Daniels, who is an EWS driver. Brian constantly gives us information to ensure we make the highest quality models. With his enthusiasm and knowledge of diesels, we have pushed modelling further than we believe possible. Modelling of this quality, standing alongside John's 'A' Shop, just has to be shown in this book. Thank you both for allowing me to use these photos.

40056

LNWR Compound

Webb must have had a sense of humour, for he called his most controversial design, his 'Problem' class. Compounding, in the late 19th century, looked as if it would be a more efficient use of steam power. Webb built some unusual locos around what looks like a 2-4-0 wheel arrangement although in fact, they are nothing of the sort. They are actually 2-2-2, both driving wheels being independent. He called the classes 'Teutonics', 'Dreadnoughts' and

'Greater Britains'. Although I couldn't have possibly seen these locomotives, they always fascinated me. There are fantastic stories of these engines having to be started with pinch bars on the driving wheels, as it was not unknown for one wheel to go one way, and the other to go in the opposite direction. But they were powerful machines and, as you can see later, the LNWR was more fascinated by compounding than most other railways.

BELOW: This shows a very typical express of the late 1890s, with a pilot engine, a 2-2-2 'Problem', and compound No 1120 *Apollo*. The leading coach is an LNWR eight-wheeler, built by John Petcher.

THIS PAGE: *Apollo* stands magnificently on its own. This is a scratch-built engine, built and painted by James Harwood in New Zealand. This was the first engine I'd seen built by James and, without question, it still totally astounds me. This is a Scale 7 loco.

THIS PAGE AND OPPOSITE: This a 10mm 'Teutonic',
No 1309 *Adriatic*, an example of the larger compound.
The smallest were the 'Dreadnoughts', then came the
'Teutonics', and the largest were the 'Greater Britains'
(these were 2-2-2-2s).

The 'Britannias' were the first BR-built main line passenger engines. I saw all of these during my spotting days and have travelled behind them more than once. They are quite striking engines to work on, but working on the real thing you do very much get the impression that even as early as 1950 Crewe knew the writing was on the wall for steam. Arguably, they only really had 10 years of service. And I can tell you first hand that they were flogged to death. In fact, all the engines that I have purchased from BR, be it steam, diesel or electric, were absolutely knackered. None more so than *Britannia* itself. When we started to take this engine apart in 2006 it was obvious that the engine had never seen any major repairs. In fact, we were all amazed to see that most of the components

were as fitted, even down to the horn dampers. When the fire box was removed from the boiler, what came to light was that when the fire box was built, the holes were in the wrong place. BR simply filled them and re-drilled them — something that would give the heath and safety experts today apoplexy.

ABOVE: No 70026 *Polar Star,* was one of the Western Region 'Britannias'. *Polar Star* was also the name of one of the first Great Western engines. Reputably, the 'Britannias' were not liked by the Western drivers. Built from a DHJ kit, painted, lined and weathered by Steve Naylor, this is one of three 'Britannias' in the collection. The picture overleaf shows a feature of BR Standards — the pipes were on the outside for ease of maintenance.

LEFT: The Western Region 'Brits' had different windshields. They had the handrail removed and had holes inserted. The 'Brits' were left-hand drive locos whereas the other Western locos were right-hand. It is claimed that the handrails obscured the signals.

OPPOSITE PAGE: This is what makes a steam engine work — the pipes that carry the water around and get the water into the boiler.

LNWR 'Claughton'

Late in the day the LNWR woke up to the fact that it desperately needed some big main line passenger engines. Crewe and Euston's attitude to money had created problems for the company but its answer was to build the 'Claughtons'. These were very big engines but, like all things in life, big is not necessarily the answer. Although they looked beautiful and powerful, they were in fact not that successful. Over the years they were rebuilt with different boilers and also fitted for oil firing. There is no question that the railway had high hopes for this class, as it carried the names of the chairman and directors of the company. The LNWR at this period in history was the world's biggest company, so they carried a lot of prestige, and you could not model the LNWR without a 'Claughton'.

THIS PAGE AND OPPOSITE: This is a Jeff Holt-built 'Claughton' with Alan Harris wheels, painted and lined by Brian Badger. This engine regularly pulls 11 clerestory coaches, and in fact has given us many hours of fun as this was the first engine used to test all of the Leamington track work.

BELOW: This engine was built for us by one of our unsung heroes from the North East, Colin Foster. He built, painted and weathered the loco. Colin is our wagon man and is responsible for all of the mineral wagons and fish traffic.

One may wonder why there is a Cambrian Railways engine in the collection. Well, every now and again, there are certain locos that catch your eye. It was not unusual to see these Cambrian engines being serviced at Wolverhampton in the '50s. I well remember No 849 pottering about and even saw it one day at Leamington Spa on a pick up goods. Their light weight allowed them to be used on the Cambrian section because of the weight restrictions. I also liked the number plates with the GWR on them. They were picked out in cream. If only at the time I had the nous to talk myself onto the footplate, I could have experienced one of these close-up.

Everybody has a favourite locomotive, and the 'Castle' class locomotives are mine. They are the best balanced engines I have ever seen. Arguably they were just an improved 'Star' class and although Collett only tinkered, this was tinkering at its best. They really were fabulous machines and anybody close to any part of the ex-Great Western railway loved these engines. All their names were splendid. They looked every inch a thoroughbred, and not until the very early 1960s did they start to look bedraggled. For the spotters like me at Leamington Spa, if their favourite wasn't a 'King', it was a 'Castle'. They went about their work with ease. One engine I hope to see restored by us before I pop my clogs is our own, No 7027 *Thornbury Castle*. One could argue that the late '50s were the 'Castles' best years, when they were fitted with improved draughting and double blast pipes. The history of the chimneys on 'Castles' is an art in itself. Even when they had double chimneys there were three types. So much for standardisation!

LEFT AND OPPOSITE: No 4073 *Caerphilly Castle* is built as 7¼-inch live steam by David Atkin. This is more perfect than the real thing. We have to use a truck to move this and in some ways, it is more difficult to steam than the real thing. But it is one hell of a piece of engineering. There is nothing on this loco that does not work properly.

THIS PAGE AND OPPOSITE: No 5054 *Earl of Ducie* is built by David Baker with Alan Harris wheels, painted by Alan Brackenborough. It is shown as it would have been seen running after 1957. I regularly saw this engine at Leamington.

GW 'Castle'

Built by George McInnon-Ure and painted by
Brian Badger this shows quite distinctly the difference
between the early outbuilt 'Castles' and the later batches.

The 'Westerns', as the Class 52s were originally called, demonstrated the Western Region's regard for itself — slightly superior to everyone else! It was decided quite early that the West Coast line would be electrified which meant that the Western Region would never be electrified. Whereas everyone else went for diesel-electrics, the Western went for diesel-hydraulics and the 'Westerns' were the pinnacle of this policy. They had two engines which meant they could, if necessary, crawl home with one. There is no question that the 'Westerns' were probably the first diesels to collect an army of followers — their noise and their shape were unique. I personally thought that the 'Westerns' looked good in any livery and in any condition, even when they started to suffer due to the carriage wash at Laira, in Plymouth.

LEFT AND ABOVE: This engine, *Western Lady*, once belonged to the Trust and the model shows engines typical of the blue period that went through the washing plant at Laira. This was built by us in the factory for an article on weathering.

THIS PAGE AND OPPOSITE: Built in our factory and painted and weathered by us, this shows one version of what we believe may have been as many as three different maroon liveries for the 'Westerns'. This is probably why so many people follow the 'Westerns'.

To the average enthusiast who likes steam engines, all diesels are boxes with wheels on. When it comes to the Class 73s, yes they are. But that is too bland a statement and too easy a cop-out. In fact, it is is a very clever compromise engine. Built by BR to run on the Southern Region, they were actually diesel electrics and were built to run on the third rail, but could run independently as diesels. They became famous in the later years for running the Gatwick Express and took the Prince Of Wales and Lady Diana on their honeymoon. I love these engines but maybe that's because I am barmy! But there is something perversely beautiful about them and, in the InterCity livery, they look brilliant. They are still around today in preservation and in use in the North West.

THIS PAGE AND OPPOSITE: This was built by Dave Lowery from an RJH kit and also painted by Dave Lowery.

Crewe always experimented — and even had the common sense to call this new design 'an Experiment'. Obvious really! The 'Experiments' were some of the oldest engines to reach Nationalisation in 1948 — they were that durable. They seem somewhat unbalanced, having inside cylinders. The great thing about all the North Western engines is when the company talked about standardisation, it meant it! If you wanted to criticise the LNWR, though, you could say that in fact its engines did look very much the same. You have to be interested enough to be able to spot the differences in tenders, but there was a common usage of things like buffers, chimneys and safety valves. The GWR made a great play of its pride in standardisation. The LNWR made no play of it, just did it!

THESE PAGES: This beautiful engine, No 306 *Autocrat*, was built by one of the best of our LNWR builders — Geoff Holt — who also painted and lined the engine. It is a truly magnificent beast! This is one of those engines that we really found difficult to justify in the collection, but because of its quality, there was no choice — it just had to be in there.

GWR 'Queen'

When studying the Great Western you soon come to the realisation that the directors were forced to go to Wolverhampton rather than that they actually wanted to go there. Right up until 1960 the Northern Division, as it was referred to by the Great Western, certainly was less important to the GWR. Although the word 'cascaded' had not even been thought of at the time, that's in effect what the Northern Division got. It was stock that was surplus to the main business. However, Wolverhampton gave the Great Western its designer William Dean, who was probably the man that put the Great into Western in engineering matters. When he left Wolverhampton, he left the factory at Stafford Road in the charge of the Armstrong family. The Armstrongs were capable railway engineers and they instituted a very pretty small passenger engine. In fact, the engine was unique — well-balanced and very much aimed at the Northern Division market, running small trains of mainly four- and six-wheeled stock between Paddington and Wolverhampton. It seems Swindon just let Joseph Armstrong get on with it and he also created the unique Wolverhampton chimneys and even painted the engines in a completely different colour. Amongst these were the 'Queen' class. These regularly pulled the Royal Train of the period. How suitable that an engine called a 'Queen' pulled the Royal Train — how typical Great Western.

RIGHT AND OPPOSITE: The loco, No 1132 *Prince of Wales*, was built by the late Harry Dumas and painted by Brian Badger. The models are 10mm scale and have sat for many years in my office as they are beautiful conversation pieces.

The 'Precedents' were Crewe's first attempt at a bigger passenger engine and you could argue, even at this early date in the 1890s, that these engines were old fashioned by that day's standards — but no-one could ever accuse the LNWR of being forward thinking! The good news is that we are lucky to have one preserved and I guess that, in itself, is a tribute to these beautifully well-proportioned engines.

RIGHT AND OPPOSITE: No 2191 *Snowdon* is built by Geoff Holt and painted by Brian Badger.

In the same way that the Great Western had a Northern Division, the LNWR had a Southern Division which was based at Wolverton and it tended to paint its engines in different colours to Crewe. When you collect LNWR engines you have to like black, unless you care to model a Southern Division engine, when you can get a green one.

The 'DX Goods' were the LNWR engines which could arguably be classified as its Class 5. This was the company's first mass-produced loco and boy were there a lot of them – over 900 were built! They lasted a long time so you can see that these were very successful engines. A distinctive feature was the double splashers allowing clearance for the rods.

THIS PAGE AND OPPOSITE: Built by Geoff Holt in 10mm and painted by Brian Badger, this shows the locomotive in its Southern Division green with castellated chimney and the early LNW smokebox door. You will notice that the loco has no brakes but, in this period, they weren't deemed necessary. The tender has wooden brake blocks and even at this early period LNWR drivers thought it unreasonable to have to stop their locos — something that lasted right up until the 1960s when LMS men would regularly remove the brake valves on the 'Super Ds'.

GWR 'River'

The 'Rivers' were beautiful little 2-4-0 locos that were regularly used in the Northern Division of the GWR. There were four, all named after rivers on the Western and one has to say they are very pretty little things. Built by the late Harry Dumas, painted by Brian Badger, No 73 *Isis* was one of the first tender locos we acquired. The 'Rivers' have sandwich frames, as did lots of these late Victorian engines. You can almost see the driver in his top hat!

ABOVE: AND RIGHT: Built by the late Harry Dumas and painted by Brian Badger, this is a 10mm model which for years sat on my desk in my office.

The LNER 'P2' is one of those locos that as a child you saw in a book and were totally fascinated by it. Not only because of its size and streamlined look, but also its name, *Cock o' the North*. They obviously were very experimental and neither Gresley nor the LNER were ever frightened to try new things out. What few people realise is that in the 1930s this attitude brought the LNER the closest to bankruptcy than any other railway ever came. It's true to say that all railways experimented but none as much as the LNER.

ABOVE: AND LEFT: This is a Korean-built loco and is therefore highly unusual to have in our collection, as it really doesn't quite fit our criteria, but because of its engineering beauty we made an exception!

The LNWR had more eight-coupled engines than any other railway. It started building them in the 1890s and they were still being built in the late 1920s. The history of these engines, though, is very complicated and we don't have space here to explain it in detail. Suffice to say that they were started by Webb as three-cylinder compounds and ended with Beames' 'G2s'. Along the way, all of the LNWR engineers put their 'four penn'orth' in with both Whale and Beames rebuilding them at some point. Even Webb was responsible for building four-cylinder compounds – as I said, the history of this class is a book in itself and if you are really interested in researching the history of the engines then you should look at Ted Talbot's book, *The London & North Western Railway Eight-Coupled Engines*. Ted is a fount of knowledge when it comes to all things LNWR and it is to him that we have to give thanks, not only for all the models in this book but also for the history of the real thing. Despite its intricate history, the one simple thing about this type is that in terms of identification, the locomotives were designated 'A', 'B', 'C', 'D', 'E', 'F' and 'G'.

THIS PAGE AND OPPOSITE: The 0-8-2 tank was built by Geoff Holt and painted by Brian Badger. We also have the 0-8-4 in the Collection.

ABOVE: This is a two-cylinder rebuild of a Webb three-cylinder Compound 'C1'.

TOP: This is a Webb four-cylinder Compound, Class B.

TOP: Top right-hand picture is a Webb three-cylinder compound Class A.

ABOVE AND LEFT: These are Whale two-cylinder rebuilds, Class C. All of the 0-8-0s on these pages were built by Geoff Holt and painted by Brian Badger or Lawrie Goddard.

THIS PAGE AND OPPOSITE: Geoff Holt's model of the Trust's 'Super D'.

49395

7F

LNWR 'Super D'

No 49395 was preserved for the National Railway Museum. It had been hidden at Buxton Shed, where it had suffered from a cracked cylinder due to a water carry over. The Trust undertook to restore the engine in 1994 to working order. This was probably one of the most complicated jobs ever undertaken in preservation. Every time we seemed to sort out one problem, we were faced with another! It took a long time but we were justly proud of the result. Although our reward was to see it once again out in full steam for all to enjoy, the London & North Western Society presented us with this model in recognition of our dedication to this engine.

49395

This is another one of those engines that we are not sure where it came from or who built it. Again, like some of the other Southern engines, we have been tempted to repaint it, but it's seen here in its LSWR livery. It's a scratch-built engine and runs very nicely. Not that these ever made it to Leamington Spa!

Here is Victorian elegance at its grandest. The Great Western decided to take four of these magnificent single engines and turn them into 4-4-0s, named after famous Great Western engineers and directors. They were spectacular! One can only think that they were an experiment to see what extra power they got from putting in one more set of wheels.

BELOW AND LEFT: Built from scratch by Peter Rolls with Alan Harris wheels and painted and weathered by Alan Brackenbrough, Peter built one of each engine — this is No 8 *Gooch*.

These were engines that for all intents and purposes were rebuilds. The boilers were from 'Dukes' and the frames from 'Bulldogs'. The Great Western called them 'Earls' but to all enthusiasts they were 'Dukedogs'. They were basically Northern Division engines and by the 1950s could be found on the Cambrian. I saw these at Leamington quite regularly in the early '50s and it was not unusual to see them in Stafford Road works. One is preserved, thanks to the guy who made those fabulous badges we all wore in the 1950s with engines on.

THIS PAGE AND OPPOSITE: This 'Dukedog' was built and weathered by Brian Caldicott and is a DJB kit.

When the Great Western decided it needed a mixed traffic engine, it was typical of Collett to put smaller wheels on his 'Saints' and call them 'Halls'. I know that this is a simplistic interpretation, but it's about as technical as we're going to get here and what it does belie is what wonderful, wonderful machines these were. What many enthusiasts don't understand is that there is a large variation within the class and of course the rebuilt engines are completely different. The modified 'Halls' were designed by Hawksworth and were influenced by the Second World War requirement of ease of manufacture with cost and maintenance being the main consideration.

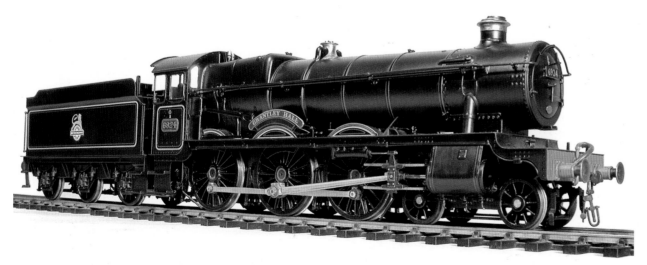

ABOVE: Here is a modified Hall, scratch built by Brian Brompton and painted by Alan Brackenborough with Harris wheels, No 6966 *Witchingham Hall*. Engines with the 'GW' writing on the tender could still be seen well into the 1950s.

LEFT: This is No 6924 *Grantley Hall* built by Paul Hanna and painted by Conrad Cooper. This was a Tyseley engine and always carried the unique all-welded 4,000-gallon tender.

OPPOSITE: This photograph shows No 4904 *Binnegar Hall* in BR Mixed Traffic Black livery. Built by Paul Hanna and painted by Conrad Cooper, it is a JLTRT Kit.

BR/LMS 'Patriot'

The one thing you can't accuse the LMS of is not getting the best out of its accounts! The 'Patriots' were originally rebuilt 'Claughtons' but the only thing that seems to have lasted from the wheel section was the wheel centres! There must have been tax relief somewhere along the line! The 'Patriots' got everywhere and lots of drivers preferred them to 'Jubilees'. They were always referred to as 'Baby Scots' by the older drivers. Their small chimneys always gave them an odd appearance and in the 1950s one even was seen with a stove pipe chimney — and that was weird. We regularly saw these around the West Midlands and Rugby always had four or five shunting about, including *Lady Godiva*.

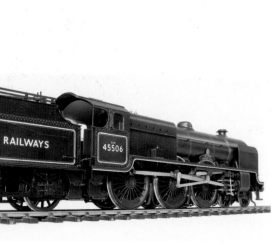

BELOW AND OPPOSITE: I bought this engine at a show of Terry Smith and it has since been re-motored but I bought it because of the 'British Rail' on the tender. It really is a fabulous little model and has not stopped working since we bought it four years ago. In fact, the reason we re-motored it is because we wore the first one out!

When it comes to elegance the 'Dean Singles' must be amongst the world's most beautiful railway engines. Designed by William Dean as the mainstay of the Victorian Great Western Railway, these were the engines that would have whisked you away from Paddington — and pretty impressive they must have looked back in the 1890s with their one large driving wheel, very ornate paintwork and huge brass domes. These were, without a doubt, very successful engines. They later even received GW tapered boilers. There was, for a while, a replica at Windsor station with one of the Royal Coaches.

OPPOSITE AND ABOVE: No 3050 *Royal Sovereign*, built by Harry Dumas, painted and lined by Brian Badger.

LEFT: No 3013 *Great Britain*, also built by Harry and painted by Brian Badger. These are the oldest engines in our collection and were built for us in 1984.

When Britain went to war in 1939 it was short of locomotives. The railway executive always knew that it would need to provide engines for not only our railways, but also for the victory in Europe. The LMS designer Riddles was brought in to design an easy to build, inexpensive loco that could be mass produced for the duration of the war and then almost thrown away, hence the name of this type — 'Austerities'. Built in Glasgow, the engines followed many LMS practices. They were not built for comfort but rather for pure power and accessibility. By the time victory was achieved, they were scattered across Britain as well as overseas and were offered to the railways at a discount. The Western took considerable numbers and both the WR and the NER made modifications to them to suit their own workshops. This was for purely practical reasons of maintenance. If you are not old enough to remember these clanking about — and clank they did — we have just finished a boiler for the 2-8-0 on the Keighley & Worth Valley Railway and it's well worth a look.

THIS PAGE AND LEFT: The modesl have Mark Wood wheels, were painted by Brian Badger and weathered by Brian Caldicott. This is version of the 2-8-0 is as operated on the Western Region with that Region's style of safety valves.

Never was there a more appropriate saying than 'It doesn't get better than this' because in my opinion it never did as far as locomotives are concerned! The 'Stars' were well thought of and the designer Churchward took the phrase 'best practice' to another level by incorporating some of the best features of locos from all over the world at this time. The GWR needed a fast-running express engine and, after short trials, got the 'Stars', 'Saints', '28XX' and 2-6-2T large tanks – now that's what I call value for money! Worthy of note is that these types were still running in some form at the end of steam on the Western Region in 1963. Anyone who has stood next to *Lode Star* in the National Railway Museum at York will have seen their beauty.

THIS PAGE AND OPPOSITE: This 'Star' is pure George Jackson Churchward. Built by George McInnon-Ure and painted by Alan Brackenbrough, this 10mm model of No 4064 *Reading Abbey* and its tender is accurate in every detail with full outside valve gear and working springs. This model shows how the First World War affected the railway, with all brass and copper removed, although the engine did hang onto the safety valve bonnet, albeit that this was over-painted.

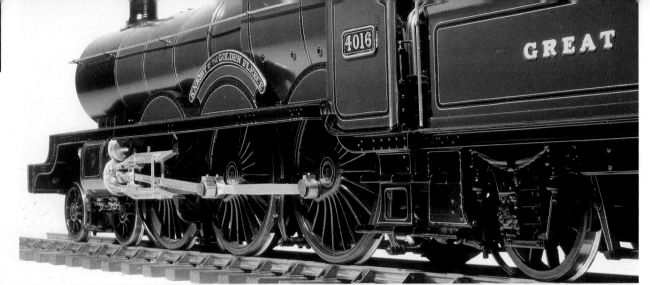

GWR 'Star'

THIS PAGE AND OPPOSITE: This is a sister engine to *Reading Abbey* and this 'Star', No 4016 *Knight of the Golden Fleece*, was built by George to show what the class was like when built in 1908 – cor!

No 4048 *Princess Victoria* was built in 1914 and, unlike No 4016, never converted to a 'Castle'.

Let's be honest – if a director came to most companies today with the broad gauge idea, he would be locked up! Not so in the 1850s, however, when the GWR thought that at 7ft 0¼in Brunel's broad gauge was a great investment. I'm glad that I never had to make a decision like that because, let's face it, to build a railway from Paddington to Cornwall was no mean feat but then only 25 years later to have it pulled up and the whole thing started again – well, words fail me! There was, however, a beauty about it in a mad way and, boy, were there some strange locos! No more so than the '35xx' 0-4-4T which not only looked strange, but did strange things! The class was used in pairs over the Devon banks and the engines were so strong that, although they did the job, they also ripped up the track!

THIS PAGE AND OPPOSITE: These are the pair that ripped up the track in Doublebois, Cornwall. Built by Bill Lee, painted and lined by Brian Badger, the drawings were scaled from the famous photo of the Swindon dump of defunct broad gauge engines by Eddie Brown.

LNWR 4-6-0

LNWR *George V* — built by Bowen-Cooke in 1909. These engines were designed for speed and, in fact, for ages were one of the classes trusted with the crack expresses of the day. It was very similar in appearance to 'Precursors'.

TOP AND RIGHT: This model was built for us by Eric Underhill and painted by Brian Badger.

This model was built by the most renowned of all 7mm locomotive builders, Stan Beeson, and is stunning. It is all scratch built and is in the collection as an example of excellence. The LNER Atlantics (ie locomotives with the 4-4-2 wheel configuration) were much followed and admired by enthusiasts. Two of this class made it into the BR era and are in the National Railway Museum.

The Western always liked to do things that were different so when the rest of BR went for diesel-electric locomotives, it went for diesel hydraulics. They took time to design them, with the result that they are fabulous to look at. The 'Hymeks' were made for picking up goods but, with lots of elements being out of the norm, they had short lives because of the difficulty in getting spares. There are three of the class still with us.

ABOVE: This is a JLTRT kit of 'Hymek' No D7068 made by us at our factory.

The pannier tanks represent the Great Western perfectly although batches of these were made by outside contractors. They were the railway's main shunters and were seen all over the system. Some had a riveted tank and No 8750 had an all-over cab. They looked really old-fashioned with their big domes. However, they worked well and still do great work – London Transport bought them from BR and so did the Coal Board so a number were preserved and we can still see them today.

THIS PAGE: GWR pannier tank No 5724 was built from start by us and painted and weathered by Steve Naylor. It just trundles around all day!

I guess because I was part owner of the *Flying Scotsman* I should have an example of the 'A3' class but it had to be one of the others so we bought this and painted it in BR livery. We can just about justify the inclusion of this LNER loco by using it on specials.

THIS PAGE AND OPPSITE: No 60096 *Papyrus* was a sister locomotive to the *Flying Scotsman*, built by Gresley for the LNER in 1928.

The one thing about all the Midland Railway engines is that they had a complete style all of their own. This model is a masterpiece! Built by James Harwood in New Zealand, it is entirely scratch built — including the wheels. Painted and lined by James, the pictures speak for themselves. It is a Scale 7 model. When James asked George McInnon-Ure to do a little bit of work on the underside of the tender George thought the work so beautiful that he did not believe that he was up to it. That is praise indeed from a craftsman such as George, and James and I were staggered by it! George was right, though — it truly is the most beautiful model ever seen.

The Class 50 diesel locomotives were built by English Electric and then hired out to BR. They were needed to fill in for the electric locomotives that terminated at Crewe and ran in pairs between Crewe and Scotland until the line was electrified; then they went to the Western Region and started to run out of Paddington. Towards the end of their lives they had a big following and I bought two for the Trust. They had lots of electronics which in turn caused lots of problems and they also smoked like mad!

RIGHT: A JLTRT kit made by us showing the appearance of the first in the class, No 50001 when it entered service.

BOTTOM: This is an old model which we bought a long time ago. It is an RJH kit of made by Dave Lowrie.

Churchward always looked at the future needs of the Great Western as his reason to build, which is why he designed the heavy freight engines later to be known as the '28XX' class. They were hugely successful and even as late as 1960 BR preferred these to any other 2-8-0 at its disposal. The '3800' was an 'Austerity' version built just before the Second World War with detail variations. With the war about to start some of the frills were taken out of the design — there being a need to save money and give easier access for maintenance.

TOP AND LEFT: Scratch-built '38XX' built by Vic Green.

The Lancashire & Yorkshire Railway 'Saddle Tanks' lasted way into BR times. I managed to see most of this class which survived into the 1950s outside the works when, as a cub, we went rambling. I'm not sure whether I enjoyed the ramble but I do know I enjoyed seeing these.

RIGHT AND BELOW: This is a Chowbent kit built for us and weathered by Steve Naylor.

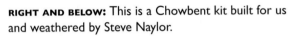

The LNWR believed in keeping things simple and no more so than in Webb's 'Coal Engines' which were literally built as a kit of parts and which, reputably, could be put together in 24 hours! These engines wandered all over the system — in fact, they wandered all over the world because the War Department used them in the First World War. They were built in very large numbers and also as a tank version. You will notice that this model, built by Geoff Holt, has the original smokebox door and no brakes! They breed 'em brave at Crewe!

These were arguably the most unsuccessful Fowler design. They certainly were poor steamers but I developed a very fond attachment to them as most were stored throughout the 1950s at Rugby by the old works. I wouldn't mind £100 for every time I've sat in them and played trains! After spending around five years in store in Rugby, they did go back into service for a short while. In reality they may have been unsuccessful, but as a model, particularly at Leamington, they are perfect.

THIS PAGE AND OPPOSITE: The models were built for us by Don Hall, painted by Conrad Cooper and they will be the basis of the Leamington-Rugby shuffles.

Index